SPACE TECH

THE HUBBLE SPACE TELESCOPE

by ALLAN MOREY

EPIC

BELLWETHER MEDIA • MINNEAPOLIS, MN

EPIC BOOKS are no ordinary books. They burst with intense action, high-speed heroics, and shadows of the unknown. Are you ready for an Epic adventure?

This edition first published in 2018 by Bellwether Media, Inc.

No part of this publication may be reproduced in whole or in part without written permission of the publisher. For information regarding permission, write to Bellwether Media, Inc., Attention: Permissions Department, 5357 Penn Avenue South, Minneapolis, MN 55419.

Library of Congress Cataloging-in-Publication Data

Names: Morey, Allan.
Title: The Hubble Space Telescope / by Allan Morey.
Description: Minneapolis, MN : Bellwether Media, Inc., 2018. | Series: Epic.
   Space Tech | Audience: Age 7-12. | Includes bibliographical references and index.
Identifiers: LCCN 2016055089 (print) | LCCN 2017006496 (ebook) | ISBN 9781626177000 (hardcover : alk. paper) |
   ISBN 9781681034300 (ebook) | ISBN 9781618912831 (paperback : alk. paper)
Subjects: LCSH: Hubble Space Telescope (Spacecraft)–Juvenile literature. | Space telescopes–Juvenile literature. |
   Outer space–Exploration–Juvenile literature.
Classification: LCC QB500.268 .M67 2018 (print) | LCC QB500.268 (ebook) | DDC 522.2919–dc23
LC record available at https://lccn.loc.gov/2016055089

Editor: Nathan Sommer   Designer: Steve Porter

Printed in the United States of America, North Mankato, MN.

TABLE OF CONTENTS

THE HUBBLE SPACE TELESCOPE AT WORK!

It is November 2008. **NASA** workers look at pictures of outer space. They were taken by the Hubble Space **Telescope**. For the first time, the workers see a planet in **orbit** around a different sun. What a discovery!

Hubble Space Telescope

Fomalhaut b Planet

2006
2004

486

OM & Sys Mgr

A FAMOUS NAME!

Hubble is named after
Edwin Hubble. He
discovered that the
universe is getting bigger!

WHAT IS THE HUBBLE SPACE TELESCOPE?

Hubble is one of the largest telescopes ever to be sent to space. On Earth, objects seen through a telescope might look blurry. Gases around Earth get in the way. Up in space, Hubble gets a much clearer view.

Hubble image of Eagle Nebula

illustration of
a black hole

Scientists use Hubble to study outer space. They have looked at **black holes** with it. Hubble has helped them find some of Pluto's moons. It has also helped spot far-off planets and stars.

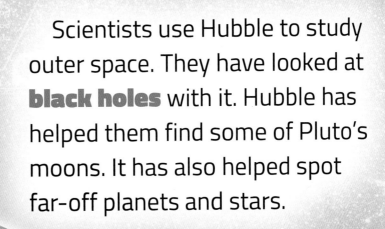

Pluto and its moon, Charon

ZIPPING AROUND!

Hubble circles Earth about once every 97 minutes.

PARTS OF THE HUBBLE SPACE TELESCOPE

Hubble works using two mirrors. A large mirror reflects light onto a smaller mirror. The smaller one reflects the light back through a hole in the larger one. This light forms an image that people can see.

Hubble photo of Whirlpool Galaxy

NASA scientists work on Hubble's mirror

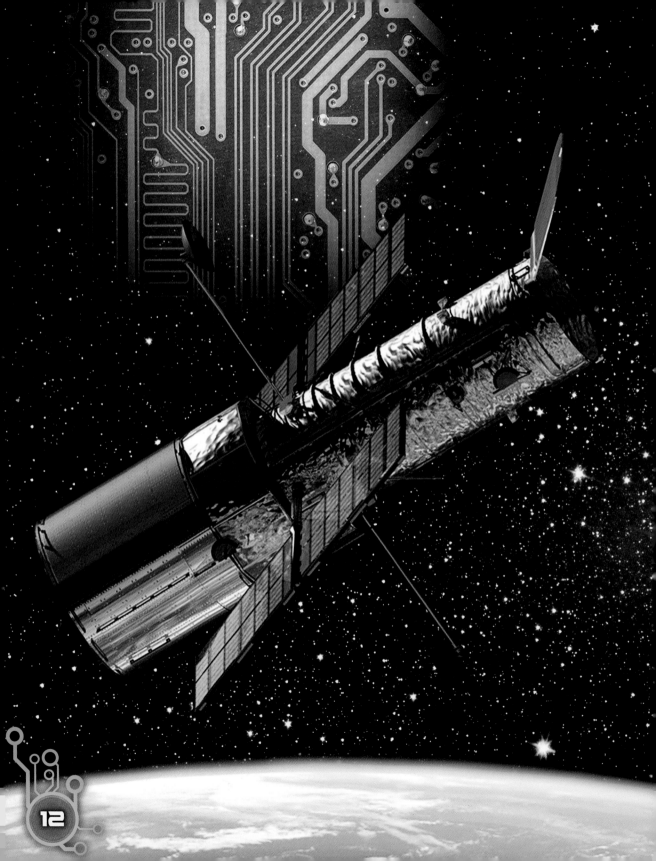

Hubble uses many tools to do its job. Cameras and **sensors** detect **ultraviolet rays**. They help measure how far objects are from Earth. They also help scientists learn what makes up these objects.

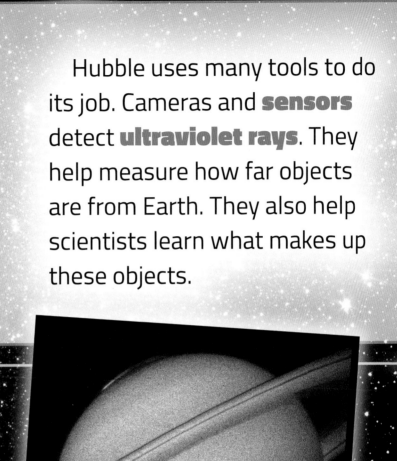

ultraviolet Hubble image of Saturn

Space is huge. Hubble's **Pointing Control System** helps scientists find what they are looking for. It turns the telescope to face whatever they want to study. **Solar panels** power Hubble.

IDENTIFY THE MACHINE
Hubble Space Telescope

- door to adjust light

- solar panels

- cameras and sensors

- Pointing Control System

- main mirror and secondary mirror

- radio antenna

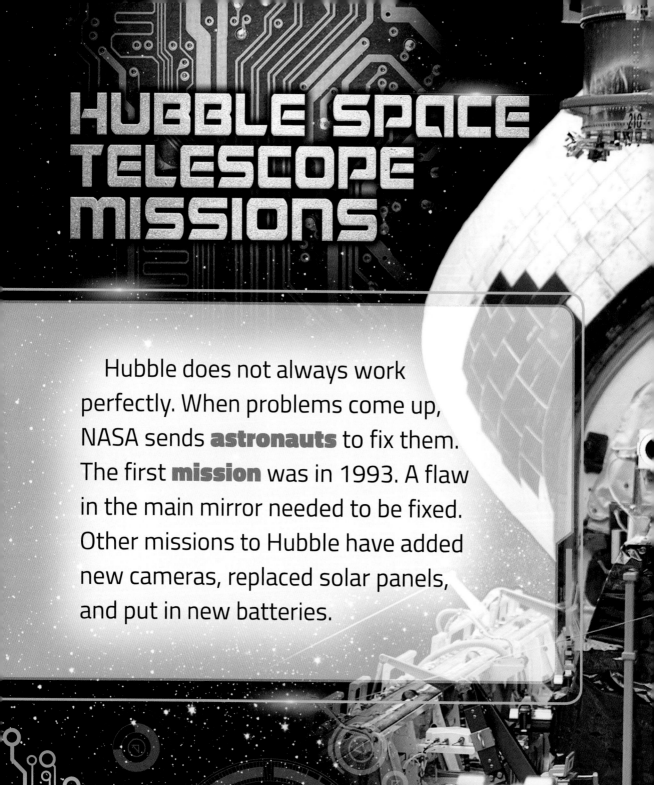

HUBBLE SPACE TELESCOPE MISSIONS

Hubble does not always work perfectly. When problems come up, NASA sends **astronauts** to fix them. The first **mission** was in 1993. A flaw in the main mirror needed to be fixed. Other missions to Hubble have added new cameras, replaced solar panels, and put in new batteries.

Hubble Space Telescope

astronaut works on the Hubble Space Telescope

Hubble has been circling Earth for about 30 years. It has helped find new planets. It has also helped discover new **galaxies**. Thanks to the Hubble Space Telescope, many secrets of space have been unlocked!

ORBITING THE SUN!

The James Webb Space Telescope is planned to launch in 2018. It will not orbit Earth. Instead, it will circle the sun.

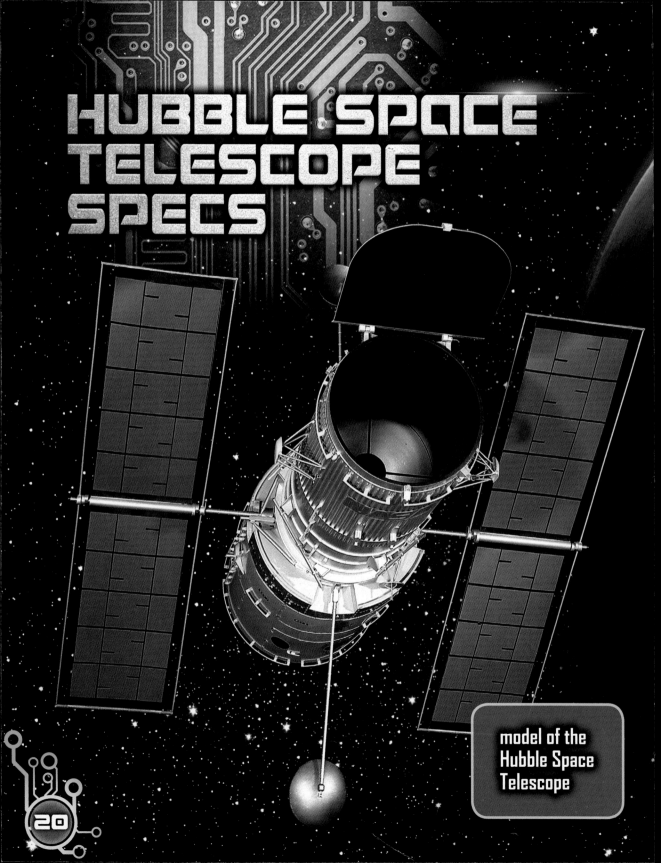

HUBBLE SPACE TELESCOPE SPECS

model of the Hubble Space Telescope

NAME: HUBBLE SPACE TELESCOPE

- mission: viewing and photographing the farthest reaches of space
- first time in space: April 24, 1990; launched into orbit from space shuttle *Discovery*.

- location in space: orbits about 340 miles (547 kilometers) above Earth
- speed: about 17,000 miles (27,359 kilometers) per hour

- maximum diameter: 14 feet (4.2 meters)

- length: 43.5 feet (13.2 meters)

GLOSSARY

astronauts—people trained to travel and work in outer space

black holes—places in outer space with incredibly strong gravity; not even light can escape the gravity of a black hole.

galaxies—large systems of stars

mission—a task or job

NASA—National Aeronautics and Space Administration; NASA is a U.S. government agency responsible for space travel and exploration.

orbit—to circle around an object

Pointing Control System—the system that controls Hubble's movements and focuses Hubble on specific targets

sensors—devices used to detect things like light, heat, and sound

solar panels—devices that collect sunlight and turn it into energy

telescope—a device used for seeing distant objects, especially those in outer space

ultraviolet rays—violet light from a star that is invisible to humans

TO LEARN MORE

AT THE LIBRARY

Cole, Michael D. *Eye on the Universe: The Incredible Hubble Space Telescope*. Berkeley Heights, N.J.: Enslow Publishers, 2013.

Kruesi, Liz. *Discover Space Exploration*. Minneapolis, Minn.: Lerner Publications, 2017.

Marlowe, Christie. *Space Telescopes*. Vestal, N.Y.: Village Earth Press, 2014.

ON THE WEB

Learning more about the Hubble Space Telescope is as easy as 1, 2, 3.

1. Go to www.factsurfer.com.

2. Enter "Hubble Space Telescope" into the search box.

3. Click the "Surf" button and you will see a list of related web sites.

With factsurfer.com, finding more information is just a click away.

INDEX

The images in this book are reproduced through the courtesy of: Denis Tabler, front cover (Hubble); NASA, front cover (Earth), pp. 4 (framed Hubble), 4-5 (planet graphic), 7 (nebula), 8-11 (all), 13 (Saturn), 14 (framed Hubble), 14-15 (Earth), 16-17, 19 (satellite), 20 (Hubble); Aphelleon, pp. 2-3; Associated Press, pp. 4-5 (Edwin Hubble); Triff, p. 6 (framed Hubble); ESA/Hubble, pp. 12-13 (Hubble/Earth), 21 (Hubble); Nerthuz, pp. 15 (Hubble), 18 (Hubble); Vadim Sadovski, pp. 18-19, 20-21 (Earth); solarseven, p. 19 (sun).